Peter Gordon is a RADA trained actor, writer and poet. Peter has enjoyed a long acting career performing at The RSC, the National Theatre and with The Peter Hall Company; as well as in film and TV. As a writer, he has had his radio plays broadcast and his stage plays performed.

A Love in Verse

Copyright © 2021 Peter Gordon

All rights reserved.

Cover image by Katie Allen Design

Curated by Anna Jordan, Cassie Davis & Lia Burge Rogers

Edited by Lia Burge Rogers

A Love in Verse

By Peter Gordon

"Here is the market place of life's events
We spend for love and do not deal in pence"

PRAISE FOR *A Love in Verse*

"Thirty years ago, "just for a laugh", actor Peter Gordon wrote a poem for his wife Alison, and left it under her pillow. She liked it, and so he carried on, every day for 25 years. To this day, Gordon continues to add to the thousands of poems he had written for Alison, even after her death four years ago."

The Guardian, Alison Flood

"The gesture is both grand and sweetly intimate, and the poems form a remarkable chronicle of domestic devotion, passion and bliss. If Peter's not the most romantic bloke alive, they suggest he's been one of the luckiest."

BBC Entertainment and Arts Website, Ian Youngs

"Nearly every day for more than 25 years Peter left a poem under his wife Alison's pillow. Here, their two daughters Cassie Davis and Anna Jordan look back on a unique love story that was hiding in plain sight all along."

The Sunday Times Style Magazine

"They describe his agony at being apart from Alison while away with work, the excitement of their reunions, the ups and downs of their relationship and the struggle he endured as a jobbing actor."

Daily Mail Online, Hayley Richardson

"I dare you to read and remain dry of cheek."

Dolly Alderton

Every day for 25 years, Peter wrote Alison a poem and put it under her pillow.

Alison died in 2016.

Peter spent six months sorting through more than 8500 poems

This is just a selection

He continues to write for her

These are his words.

INTRODUCTION

In 1972 *The Half Moon Theatre* was a dingy 'fringe' venue in the East End of London. For their first production they settled on an early Brecht piece, *The Jungle of the Cities*. The cast consisted of eleven men and three women, one of whom would turn out to be my future wife, Alison.

We had no scenes together, minimal contact during rehearsals and the run of the play, and no reason to spend any of our free time together. Besides, I was married and she had a boyfriend. From what little impression we did make on each other, I concluded that she was rather a sad figure and she thought me (to quote from a poem I wrote years later) 'brash, overconfident, lost indeed.' Such was our inauspicious first meeting.

Over a year later, casting was taking place for a different play. This one was new – a first effort in fact – with a small cast of three, and was to take place at the *Traverse Theatre* in Edinburgh. The play was called *Plat du Jour*, in which an estranged husband returns home to his wife, with his male lover in tow. Throughout the course of the play they eat her limb by limb, served up in various dishes (the author had recently been through a bad break up). I had auditioned for the role of the husband, and Alison had auditioned for role of the wife. We both got the parts.

We started rehearsals in 1973. By now my marriage and her relationship had both come to an end. She thought I was as arrogant as ever; I thought she was maybe a little gloomier than before. Nevertheless, to save money on rent I suggested we look for digs that were in effect one flat but with two bedrooms. She agreed and we found such a place.

For a few days we moved warily around each other, unsure what to make of the situation. We avoided each other as much as possible. With massive parts to learn, what was more reasonable than to sit in our respective rooms studying our lines alone?

We inevitably got to talk a little. I found that she was intelligent and had good taste. We discovered an old-fashioned milk bar in Edinburgh – these had since died out in London – and would visit it on our way back from rehearsal.

Back at our digs things became friendlier too. Once we were familiar with our parts it made sense to go over our lines together. We got to talk about ourselves more and imperceptibly opened up to each other. The single cooker in the flat happened to be in my room, so at first, we would cook individually. Eventually (and thankfully) it led to her preparing one meal for the both of us (she was a far better cook than me!). We talked about our lives, our dreams, our previous relationships, our families; Alison told me about her two children from her previous marriage. We connected.

One evening, not long before the opening night, I was collecting the dishes to wash up and we found ourselves face-to-face. It seemed somehow natural, though heart-seizing, to kiss and embrace. No more concealment – we had discovered each other, vulnerable and hurt by the past maybe, but open and undisguised to each other.

Once *Plat du Jour* opened we had the days free to amuse ourselves. We were happy lovers, the show was bringing guests in, and Edinburgh was pleasant in the spring. After rising late we would spend the afternoon doing touristy things, head off to perform the play in the evening, and afterwards eat voraciously at the restaurant above the theatre (their signature dish was cow's brains – and we loved every last morsel!). Our final performance was on the 1st July, Alison's 32nd birthday, and the following day we travelled on the train back to London together. On that journey we talked seriously about our future lives and decided they would be spent together.

Seventeen years later I was sitting at my desk in the bay window of our bedroom, looking out onto Mafeking Avenue in Brentford. I thought about this beginning to our relationship and all of the things that had happened since. An extraordinary series of events had led to two broke actors owning a charming Victorian house. Here, Dominic and Karen - Alison's older children - resided before going off to university and settling into the flat next door, respectively. And here we lived now with our daughters, Cassie and Anna. I thought about their births, and how they had overcome serious illnesses early on in their lives. Our love had remained steadfast throughout the years. But I was out of work (the acting profession not being a particularly stable one) and I worried that I couldn't provide. We had just returned from a rare and long-awaited holiday, summer was nearing at an end and we all felt a little bleak, especially Alison. The least I could do, I suddenly thought, would be to assure Alison, my wife of sixteen years, of my love and devotion to her and our family. Not verbally – I was always doing that anyway – but in writing. A little note; a token, so to speak. So, I found an old scrap of paper and wrote:

My love / It never stops / But it changes / New things every day / All wonderful

I crept upstairs and placed it under her pillow. That night, she read it quietly, saying nothing but her smile widening. "Read it out loud to me" she asked. And so I did. It was sincere and basic. "Again" she said. I read it again, slightly awkwardly. "It's just a little thought" I said as I gave it back to her. Still smiling, she read it through silently to herself, then looked at me, her eyes glistening. "No one's ever written anything like that for me before". She returned it to its place under her pillow and smiled at me once more.

And so, just like that, I started to leave a note for her every night. I started to get a little more creative and began introducing rhymes into the messages, and finally they became fully formed poems.

The development of my poetry, I can only describe as organic. I wrote the poems anywhere and everywhere: on tour in my digs, in the dressing room backstage, on trains, planes and buses, and often on scraps of old script she could always turn over to, if she tired of my verse.

The decades that followed were content and loving; full of joy but pain and sadness too - such is life.

Twenty-five years after that first silly verse was written, my beloved Alison was diagnosed with lung cancer. As we left the doctor's office after getting the fatal prognosis, she whispered to our daughter Cassie: "You will look after him, won't you? He can come and live with you?" Even at the worst of times she was always thinking of me. She died just eighteen months later.

I did move in with Cassie after Alison's death. I had a lot of belongings; memories from our full and happy life together – so I deposited them in the shed at the bottom of her garden. In late spring 2017, I was sitting in there having a sort out and came across the thousands of scraps of paper with writing on them – the poems I'd written daily to her from 1990 to her death in 2016. Looking through them I thought that though often hastily composed, some of them were reasonably well written. I spent months out there in that shed, getting through countless cups of tea and glasses of beer, sorting through them quite ruthlessly. I came up with about three hundred of the several thousand there, which – dare I say it – I thought were quite good. I showed them to my daughters Anna and Cassie who loved them.

They thought that other people might like to read them too. I wanted to share these poems to commemorate our Alison, who we knew as a wonderful wife, mother and human being. And so, *A Love in Verse* was born.

In its first incarnation, it was an online selection of the best poems www.aloveinverse.com. Between them, the girls did everything (I being quite ignorant about those technicalities). They hired an expert to build the website and it has proved a success, with publications such as *The Guardian, BBC, The Sunday Times Style*, and podcast *The High Low* featuring our story. We've also had a number of actors record videos of the poems – several that we'd both worked with over the years, and many of Alison's students that she'd taught at drama school, where she happily spent the later years of her career. I'm told the website has been very popular, as are the social media accounts, all having thousands of visitors. A poetry group chose these poems to discuss at their weekly meeting, and an English teacher in Germany has studied them with her class.

As the fondness of our memories of Alison grew, so did the desire to celebrate her more widely. And so, we decided to immortalise a selection of these poems into a book. I want the world to know about Alison – my Allie. Whatever the artistic merits of the poetry, I believe it does reveal the depth of our reciprocal love and my huge appreciation of her tenderness, intelligence, talents, kindness and concern for others. Above all else, this is a story of enduring love. This is for you, Allie.

CONTENTS

CHAPTER 1 – GLORIOUS LOVE

Neither Alison nor I expected to fall in love while working together in Edinburgh. We'd both recently come out of long-term relationships, and at 31 and 40 respectively, we'd accrued enough experience of love to be wary of it! But they say that love happens when you least expect it, and thankfully fate intervened and put Alison and me in the right place, at the right time.

This chapter charts the headiness of early love through to that deeper, settled devotion between two people who know each other inside out. Despite neither of us being spring chickens there was something wonderfully 'studentish' about the way Alison and I got together - in digs, with a shared cooker in one room, and very little money.

We felt in finding each other we were finally able to find ourselves – or the people we were meant to be. There was a strong feeling of security and trust, affording us not only comfort and intimacy; but the opportunity to explore life and the world outside of our relationship – without any feelings of jealousy or resentment.

By the time I started writing Alison a poem every day in the 1990s, we'd been together nearly twenty years. Our love was as intense, but had mellowed into something deeper and more mature. As the years passed, I never lost that deep sense of wonder that she was mine.

Edinburgh

I sing an Edinburgh song:

Of love in bed all morning long,

(We never made that lunchtime show)

The castle garden's where we'd go,

And eat ice cream and pitch and putt;

The brains on which we'd mighty glut;

Being together in a play;

We're together every day;

Together touring Princes Street,

And having fun at Arthur's Seat.

I sing an Edinburgh song,

For you, my love, all my life long.

Wot a Girl

She climbs in the car

Fag in mouth and hair in wind

Fiddles with the door and waves

Having caught my eye.

Returns, complaining "cold"

Black trousers, karate jacket

Finds a scarf and has a word

Goes back to the car

And I think "never say die"

I've Tried to Write a Poem

Our eyes met this morning, our very

Minds and souls seemed to join and everything

To be said was said and past and present and future

Were contained there

And I thought – maybe I tried to say –

That if we could spend all our moments,

Together or apart in the trust of these seconds

When everything of love was totally open

We'd be strong enough for everything

We'd be ok. And we will be.

By the Aegean

Three boats ride at anchor in the calm night

Warning lights winking without respite

And the far headlands to left and right

Harbour the sea

Lapping under where we

From our balcony

Watch for the dawn

Ouzo that clouds when water's poured in

Cigarettes in the half dark as dawn's sighs begin:

The streaks in the east and that rattling din

Of fishing boats, early

Skies become pearly

Dawn with my girlie

By the Aegean.

28th March 1998

Hair Wash

I looked in, saw you washing your hair,

Kneeling, turning head side to side

To catch the shower jets, eyes tight shut

Arms, shoulders bare. I've loved you so much.

You looked so vulnerable. I dare not speak

For fear to frighten you but closed the door,

Came, sat before the daffodils you placed for me.

A vast passion forms in me, passion of tenderness

Consumes me, I hunger to love you too much

But must leave you space.

One Fine Hand

I remember pigeons and sparrows

On the green beneath Edinburgh Castle

I remember smoking a secret joint

In a house where a policeman was visiting

I remember holding your fevered hand

The night that our first child was born

I remember wood fires in a cottage

Drinking cider, the two girls asleep

I remember a magnificent dawn

In Greece, sipping ouzo, smoking fags

In the game of remembrance I've many good cards

And this, just one fine hand to play.

31stAugust 1999

<u>Still in Bud</u>

Summer's last day it might be said

Holidays end, soon schools return

Then for another spring we yearn

As the windblown leaves grow red.

Surprise, surprise! Guess what I'm saying:

In lovers' hearts summer goes on

And no sad leaves descend upon

A resigned earth – our game's still playing.

Each kiss is worth a sunlit day

A hand's clasp keeps the flowers growing

To bed and to the beach we're going

Our skins turn gold in days of grey.

Embraces clothe us from the cold

Joy still in bud as the year grows old.

<u>All I Want</u>

We sit opposite at the table

You have reached your hand to mine

They clasp

You look towards one window I to the other

Tho' sun has graced the gardens and obtrudes

Happily into our large kitchen.

The middle of Sunday afternoon and peaceful

The tape of Richard Strauss' *Morgens*

Fills the room with Janet Baker

Barbirolli and the Hallé

The song tells of sunny mornings

Walking down to a beach

We are together listening in thrall

To perfection.

I look at you likewise in thrall

To a kind of human perfection

That's all I want on earth.

CHAPTER TWO – LONGING

Both being actors, Alison and I would often spend weeks or months apart while one or other of us was touring in a play, away rehearsing, or on location filming. There's a lot of time spent 'hanging around' when you're on set, and long days to fill when you're waiting to perform a show in the evenings - so plenty of time for poetry writing! I wanted her to know that even when apart, I was always thinking of her.

The poems in this chapter are about how much I missed Alison during those partings, and the happiness I felt on returning home to her – even if I'd only been away for a day. I always took comfort in the knowledge that at some point we'd be reunited, and happier times were waiting just around the corner.

Moscow Nights

Moscow nights are minus one

Moscow days have lots of fun

A certain amount of painful fun

(A subway system second to none)

But Moscow nights are minus one

Moscow nights are minus you

Moscow days without you too

Quite a lot of things to do

(The Kremlin's worth an hour or two)

But Moscow! Moscow's minus you

I turn my heart each Moscow day

Where sixteen hundred miles away

I left my love where two girls play

And more than tired rhymes can say

I miss my loves each Moscow day.

Coming Home

When coming out into the evening air

The sky is filled with promise, blue or clouded

The streets are joy, the bus beyond compare

The train's a train to heaven however crowded

The bus-stop this end's a fantastic haven

The sixty-five (when it arrived) a dream

The Lion Red's a rocking pub to rave in

And Mafeking has paradisiacal gleam

As for our house, which is the place of places

As for our hall, our kitchen, everywhere

As for the ravishing wonder of your faces

Cassie and Anna, Alison ma chère

Words cannot offer even the faintest clue

Of what it's like just coming home to you

A School for Scandal

All week I've worn this wig and dress

And watched the camp convoy of scandal pass

And asked "For such fey art could I care less

Strutting on heels, so far from my dear lass?"

There's just one curtain-up I want to see –

Two lids rising above two marvellous eyes

The world's no stage but just a set for me,

A background for the two blue stars I prize.

I'd take the littlest part, however mean,

So long as you are with me in the scene.

<u>Wolverhampton</u>

The same old questions – where to eat?

What shall I do from now till then?

Somewhere in England rise again

In a life that's half complete,

Wandering from theatre to theatre –

Which may be worse, which may be better.

Down Lichfield Street, the lights turned on

For Christmas glow against a sky

That's dusty orange – a coloured sigh

For that late autumn sun just gone.

It's merry, lovely; shan't complain

Or sing "I miss you" once again.

(cont)

Each sparkling light is just for you,

That fond rich autumn sky as well,

The busy bus, the bright shops tell

Those tales of which I've written a few!

Of lovers who, though kept apart,

Live together in one heart.

An Ideal Husband

I feel my life blessed by your love

I sit here in a radiant sun

Reminded of you, warmth above,

All round, with yours within made one.

And from a train, the Thames, the trees,

Appearing perfect in their grace

Share their lovely power to please

With the heaven of your face.

And even when I play my part

And hear (I hope!) the laughter swell

I tell the audience in my heart

"That laughter is for her as well"

17th February 1999

<u>Away on Tour</u>

Darkness tumbles from the flies

And fills the gloomy wings

Your backstage lover sits and sighs

Remembering many things

The thousand hours we're apart

The few we are together

Loneliness – your lover's heart

Almost beyond its tether

The leading actor loud on stage

Impresses in his part

I do mine for a weekly wage

And not for love of art.

16th December 2011

<u>Absence</u>

The leaves hang low now with the weight of summer,

Swallow you up along the sun-flecked path

Only your legs I see (heart like a drummer!)

Green finally enfolds you – gone from the hearth

This home's a world now wounded by your absence

Pictures hang sad as flowers in the vase

Bees buzz mournful in the garden's pleasance

The cats imagine that you've gone to Mars

My other world, your heart, is likewise wounded

Your sighs announced it as we kissed goodbye

The leaving hurting as the Beatles' tune did

That we played briefly, watching moments fly

There's no good reason though why hearts should break –

It's just a dental check-up, for heaven's sake!

CHAPTER 3 – DOMESTIC LIFE

In my younger years the idea of 'settling down' was abhorrent to me, I wanted success as an actor and ploughed my energies into that until my early forties. The idea of domestic life as staid and dull, changed when I met Alison. She showed me that it could be full of wonder and small moments of joy. This chapter is a tender celebration of domesticity.

These poems chart mine and Alison's happy, humdrum life together; without shying away from the realities of love. Like so many, we had money worries and serious illnesses to contend with; but loving relationships make even the most difficult situations easier to bear.

27th May 1992

<u>Seeking You</u>

Here in the marvellous garden

The magic shadows play;

With the sunlight's pardon

They entertain the day.

Flowers, fewer yet shining

The black cat blinks in the shade;

Each thing underlining

The beauty you have made.

Here are two that miss you, both

Ardent lovers true

I, and from the undergrowth

A gnome peers, seeking you.

Schubert

Already I've forgotten what you wore

Sunday, standing by the fridge; it was black,

And your arm supported the broom you were

About to use; but I remember

The studied intensity about your brow and eyes

As with hand gracing

The air before your face you conducted

Schubert's B flat Sonata played by Brendel

If there were reincarnation

Through a thousand lives I would remember

Those moments when I saw into

The soul most lovable whom I most love.

<u>Where Love Belongs</u>

We live in a wild tangle: spider plants,

Joy, easy chairs, their day long had,

A plethora of cats, daughters that dance

Lose things and watch the box and love their Dad,

Rooms that are pastel pink and blue and green,

Corners where cherished cobwebs fear no broom,

Gnarled table-legs where cats' long claws have been.

And nooks where shadows spread a friendly gloom,

Fine ancient bric-a-brac chosen with care

Long shelves of books well-loved and worn, a Mum

Whose young heart has a part in all that's there,

Without whom home and all the world is glum,

Her garden! Filled with flowers singing songs

Of our wild tangled home where love belongs.

The Cause

From kitchen to the garden, from the garden to the skies

This is my world of Thursdays where you, the very moon,

Irradiate the evening with gleaming of your eyes,

Become my sun in daylight to fire the afternoon

From hallway to the bedroom, from bedroom to your heart

Ecstatically mine travels; your presence everywhere

(For I can hear you singing) invades each blessed part

Excites the very cobwebs, gives happiness to air

I come to you, I put my hands in yours

That I hold life as heaven – you are the cause.

<u>Old Brentford Home</u>

I see you solo in the shadowy house

You move from room to room, you stroke a cat

You listen to a tape (it could be Strauss –

Richard of course). I wish that we could chat

Later we will, and smile and drink and kiss –

All the ingredients of a lovers' evening there

In the old 'distressed' home I daily miss

We'll find; memories and music everywhere

Love in the corners, care upon the stair

You stripped, fondness in photos, theatre bills;

Our house – a world of experience we share,

Shutting out a universe of many ills

Sunday, tomorrow, the family dinner

Our smashing home, really is a winner!

Owning the World

In terms of worldly achievement, no,

Not an impressive report to make:

Like, nothing published, whilst long ago

His acting hopes burnt at the stake.

(Not even the ashes left.) He looks

Round at a bed behind him there

And sees a world of love – the books

He didn't write cause him no care –

For there his love sleeps gently curled

Cat at her feet cleaning its face

He knows at once he owns the world

His life is bigger than all space.

The Love That Lights

Roar away my feisty snorer

Whilst I leave to have a pee

What could frighten an adorer

Lover of all aspects, like me?

Not that noisy serenading

Nor the stirring in the trees

I would hate to hear them fading –

Nature, nasals, they all please.

Branches weaving, roaming, catch the

Morning sun but that good blaze

Can't surpass or even match the

Love that lights you all my days.

Life Blessed

The sweet peas that she gathers

Are destined for some jar

She walks the garden, scissors in hand

Not going (I'm glad) far

She's back within the house now

And I can only hear

Suggestions of her presence

Which is to me so dear

This woman who's so precious

You see's my key to life

A life that's heaven despite the blows

Because she is my wife.

Mem'ries

Remember that time we sat out

With coffee, doing lists?

Filled with contentment and without

A care? Gone in the mists

Of Time, that time, it's further than the moon

Hold on – what? It was just this afternoon!

Another occasion in the garden too

You do the beds, I'm mowing the lawn

Marvelling again at how the pansies grew

And flowers glorious as the dawn

Will it occur again one day?

You bet – tomorrow, that's Sunday

My love, my love, how dare we suffer sorrow

With such mem'ries of today and tomorrow?

CHAPTER 4 – LOVE AND CONFLICT

Real love, like the kind Alison and I shared, is far from the romantic ideal often sold in films and books. Unfortunately, life often gets in the way! These poems explore that sense of disquiet that comes when you've argued with a loved one; but also acceptance, acquiescence, and the relief of making up.

Unless you're very successful, acting rarely pays well. We were under constant financial strain, which would cause us to be tetchy with one another and pick fights over the little things. I would often be away for work, leaving Alison at home to hold the fort with two small children. She felt trapped, thwarted and resentful; I didn't understand. Writing poems during an argument always felt cathartic – a chance to process my anger. There were small arguments – and mighty rows. But one of us would always yield before too long, and cross words were often undone with a cup of tea or a fleeting kiss on the top of the head.

Sonnet

Flowers and love songs are expected things

And verse like this (but better) when the talk

Concerns romantic love but let's not baulk

To mention rougher happenings life brings

To love whose romance has the depth of ours –

The rows, the bloody screams, momentary hate

The sweat getting and raising kids, the wait

For work to come, no cash, the way hope sours

No problem! Sounds a lot but just a sauce.

To the great ten course meal which we two share

What would love be without the cause to care,

Occasional pain, forgiveness, even remorse?

Here is the market place of life's events

We spend for love and do not deal in pence.

3rd July 1999

<u>Antibodies</u>

I hurt my heart in hurting you

It goes both ways I guess

Two hearts are wounded but it's true

Both hearts have the power to bless

And knit together wounds that gape

To banish scars and restore shape

Love's antibodies are so strong

That hurt can never live for long.

Lostness

A variation in your voice

One decibel from your tender-loving

And I'm lost, leaning in my seat

Forward, eyes on nothing.

The air is heavy all the day

I depend on you for breath.

Free me to breathe, help me to live

Let me laugh before I die.

I bring a cylinder of stars,

Pour them on your head, I scoop

My heart up from the gutter, give

A brush and offer it again.

The Beautiful Team

I love the times you call me a cunt

Though some might think it an affront

But I still bliss in knowing this:

Behind each cunt word is a kiss,

Each savage swearword hides a song

Of love to tell me I belong

Belong to the beautiful team called Us

Where there's not disharmonious fuss

But realisation, and the fact

That our encounter was an act

Made in heaven, or something like

Where love's in power and hate's on strike

So, darling darling it's no stunt

Nor are you being unfairly blunt

When you say (I love it) "cunt"

<u>Chilly Man</u>

We'd had bad words but now were fine

In the night she went to pee

Muttering something, the tone a sign

That she felt angry still. "Can't see"

I thought 'what words could properly calm

Her now? She needs a loving arm

When she comes back I will embrace

Fiercely but tenderly, her form –

Pressed close my warmth will leave no space

For angst – like safety from a storm.'

Unthinkingly, when back in bed

She arched her back at me instead

(cont)

Unreachable. I turned away

Hopeful at least of decent sleep

But found the bedclothes churned away

So craftily I tried to creep

The covers back – a sound within her

Like a lion disturbed at dinner!

What's left of my romantic plan?

A disappointed, chilly man.

<u>Sonnet: We Argue</u>

We Argue – harmony has some bum notes

Uninterrupted bliss is not our scene

My poems suggest our love has nothing mean

Or bad about it – joy gets all the votes

To reach that far we'd both have to be saints

By definition saints cannot be married

A saint without you? I'd rather be buried

So let's have love with no holy restraints

We're human and we love as humans do

Coming together sometimes gives off sparks

And in the light we see how passion arcs

From bright to storm and back our whole life through.

The storms are few and frankly give a sauce

To love and living it without remorse.

No Notes

Forgive long days when no notes come

I feel the lack as well as you –

Something creative and honest to do –

I fear you'll feel my love's struck dumb,

But, no, I love you on and on

And on till time itself is gone

This love affair with you I must

Honour in deed and word and verse

Always – thoughts of your eyes I'll nurse,

Your marvellous hair, your looks – discussed

Within these lines a million times

In silly, earnest, well-meant rhymes –

Forever

CHAPTER 5 – GOODBYES

Alison was diagnosed with lung cancer in October 2014. The prognosis was bleak and the doctor told us that the average patient with Alison's stage of cancer would survive four to six months. It was an utter shock; a body blow. The four of us hugged outside the hospital – there were no tears, not yet. Later we sat around at home drinking tea, trying to come to terms with what we'd heard; but also trying to carry on as normal. I remember doing the Guardian crossword, and Allie acing clue after clue, on top form. It seemed so strange considering how ill she was at that point. She seemed completely normal, our Allie.

The only reason I am able to relay the details of what was said in the doctor's office is because my daughters have told me. Strangely, I completely blocked the day's events out. I knew Alison was very ill, and that one day she would die from cancer – but that brutal time frame completely evaporated from my mind. It was as though it was so unbearable, that my brain behaved in such a way that I didn't have to bear it.

Allie had several rounds of chemo. Though it was traumatic, I have fond memories of us getting the bus or a taxi up to the hospital and me being there by her side through every step. It felt like me and her against the world. Throughout this time I continued to write, of course. I never dwelled very much on the cancer in the verses, just the odd mention of it here and there. But really, the poems were as they had always been – about our deep love and our little routines and habits. Those things don't change. I had four decades of wonderful life together to draw on. I was never going to run out of things to say.

Allie being ill gave me more opportunities to express my love through caring for her. And in fact, she lived for another eighteen months in total. The children visited more and more, we took a holiday and had two wonderful Christmases.

As the chemo progressed Allie's spirit remained bright, but it really took its toll physically. Still, it was a shock when she was rushed into hospital on the 9th May 2016 and we discovered she had pneumonia.

In fact, just the day before I had written her a poem whilst waiting to get my hair cut. All was well; all was normal. She deteriorated quickly. It was clear that we did not have long, but we were immensely lucky that she was in no pain and being taken care of by wonderful doctors and nurses. She was heavily sedated and my daughters tell me that the last words she said to them before slipping into unconsciousness were "Is daddy alright?"

She died twenty-four hours later with all of us around her. As she took her last breath I had a strong sense that she was saying to me "stay in touch."

I wrote a lot of poetry for Allie after she died. Perhaps it was a release. Perhaps it was a way of staying in touch, as I had promised I would. The strange thing was that I didn't have anyone to give them to, so I started to send them to my daughter Anna who is a writer herself, and she sent me some of her own poetry about Alison in response. It was a comfort in a strange and desolate time.

I don't think I need to write poems to keep Alison alive for me. I feel she is with me, always, giving me guidance and comfort and love – just like she always did. The poems I write for her now are a ritual of love, a reminder of how lucky and joyous my life has been. And I believe – even now – she loves to receive them.

Acceptance

For every joy there comes a pain;

To know you's joy – and your demise?

The thrilling kiss, the soul that cries…

Let's fasten seat belts, face it plain:

That you might leave me years to mope

Before I come, meet you in heaven…

Do we BELIEVE? There's other leaven

To the loaf – the leaven's Hope

Belief I force upon my mind –

It roots not well, but hope's the thing

To joy and pain the bridge I bring.

Belief is harsh but hope is kind.

I hope for God. I hope for you.

Each means always. Hope is true.

Diagnosis Day Plus Ten

When the stars go home at dawn

And the moon shuts up his shop

When hunting owls caught on the hop

Treeward on grey wings are borne

My romance is deep asleep

And I in dreams her company keep

Likewise, when the sun's abroad

And traffic roar invades the sky

We'll be wandering, she and I,

The Kentish streets in sweet accord

For each other we adore

And could not love each other more

In thickest night or radiant sun

Asleep, awake, our hearts are one.

8th April 2016

<u>Caring for You</u>

Why do I love you?

Because stars stand in the sky

And never seem to die

My love's like that too

The tide ebbs in, flows out

And Pete's always about

Caring for you all he can

And helping you as you go

There's no other way that I know

I'm always your man

I'm sorry if that sounds a boast

Most other men could have me for toast

But for whom else would I care?

I open my eyes, you are there.

Chemo

I look at you asleep in the dim

Dining room's post meridian gloom

And think, how fortunate is this room

To have her there youthful and slim –

On her bunched fingers her sweet chin rests

Whilst every side-effect she bests

None can taunt with "You can't win"

Her fighting strength is at its peak

For though she slumbers she's not weak

She's restoring – beneath her skin

Are all those years surviving me –

What greater challenge could there be?

Our prayers go up to God above

Buoyed up with the strength of our love.

The Last I Wrote While She Was Still Alive

The air is grey but the temperature's warm

Late afternoon in an old Kent town

My mood is neutral, kind of brown –

Suddenly feel that it might storm

And I've no brolly but never mind

On the whole I feel fate's been kind

Who minds getting wet when you've got a Rose

A treasure, a pleasure past all dreaming?

The sun might just as well be beaming

Everything's gleaming where she goes

The world transformed is my life with my Allie

Come dark or distress she'll always rally

Oh, let it soak me to the skin

I'll soon be home – and she'll be in.

The Cedar Room

The hospital has the Cedar Room

Where visitors may go to rest

From watching the very sick, oppressed

By memories of them in their bloom

Who now decline in short-breathed sleep;

The Cedar Room's to rest – and weep.

But I don't go there, afraid to tear

My gaze from that dear, much loved face

Of her whom I'll no more embrace -

Oh God, that thought is hell to bear

For heaven is when she's everywhere

And hell is when is she is not there

But now she's gone and all is gloom

And all the world's a Cedar Room.

Maybe Blue Skies

I miss you love at evening time

On a day of endless rain

Out on your garden I gaze again

(Every bud green in the gloom)

And recall you in your prime

Gentle and eager, tending each bloom

Rains ended and the birds all sing

Sweet and tuneful, bright and alive,

Announcing to the world, "We thrive –

Though suns decline they will arise"

And asking, "What will a new dawn bring?"

Maybe new hope, maybe blue skies –

But never as blue as the blue of your eyes.

The Missing Poem

It's good to stride out with your lover at dusk

The sky is still luminous with purple clouds drifting

And we're feeling spry for our spirits are lifting

And all that remains of our sorrow's the husk.

She hangs on my arm or we go hand in hand

And we chat – well, she's sending me up half the time,

Or we're making up songs and trying to rhyme

And laughing sometimes when the words haven't scanned.

Well, we get to the place and buy what we came for

And start to walk back – when I somehow forget

That she's with me and I feel such shame and regret,

But she says, oh my love, you have nothing to feel blame for,

Even the fondest, it can't be denied,

May forget now and then – it's a year since I died.

<u>The Old Piano</u>

The tears I'd gladly pay

To hear you play once more!

– I shed them anyway

Each time I listen for

Your fingers on the keys-

The thought can only tease

The rain may fall all day

The sun burn up the blue

The years may fall away

(They'll lead me nearer you)

But always I'll recall

Singing down the hall

(cont)

That perfection of tone

And sometime hesitation

That was your very own

An almost meditation

On the pain and sweetness

When love seals life's completeness

<u>What Makes Sense</u>

Though seasons turn it shan't be hard

To see those last years out

Must find things different, catch them starred

By wonder and not doubt

The glories of the universe

Are mine, should I desire

To exalt in or to rehearse

A world of joy and fire

And memories of your kiss, your love,

These last are what remains

Of life's adventures far above

So much my heart disdains

(cont)

For there is only you, you, you

Though heaven itself presents

You are the wonder, the most true,

Life at its most intense –

Finally, what makes sense

I Shall Not Hold You Again

In life I shall not hold you again -

I've held the box your ashes are in -

But I can't take death on the chin

Or moon about 'remember when'

For I've your picture by my side

Caught in a flash of happiness-

Saying 'Get Lost!' to all distress

With shining eyes and a smile so wide

But more than consolation, this

For me, is a focus on your spirit

And not just hope alone is in it

Or a memory of bliss;

Above all these your strength is there

To lift me up and bid me dare

We'd love to hear your thoughts on *A Love in Verse*.

Do email us at aloveinverse@outlook.com

Printed in Great Britain
by Amazon

65127275R00040